Wild Weather

Blizzard

REVISED AND UPDATED

Catherine Chambers

www.heinemann.co.uk/library
Visit our website to find out more information about **Heinemann Library** books.

To order:
- ☎ Phone ++44 (0)1865 888112
- ▤ Send a fax to ++44 (0)1865 314091
- ⌨ Visit the Heinemann Bookshop at www.heinemann.co.uk/library to browse our catalogue and order online.

First published in Great Britain by Heinemann Library, Halley Court, Jordan Hill, Oxford OX2 8EJ, part of Harcourt Education. Heinemann is a registered trademark of Harcourt Education.

Editorial: Clare Lewis
Designed: Steve Mead and Q2A
Illustrations: Paul Bale
Picture Research: Tracy Cummins
Production: Julie Carter

Originated by Modern Age Repro
Printed and bound in China by South China Printing Company Limited

10 digit ISBN 0 431 15082 6
13 digit ISBN 978 0 431 15082 6

11 10 09 08 07
10 9 8 7 6 5 4 3 2 1

British Library Cataloguing in Publication Data

Chambers, Catherine
Wild Weather: Blizzard. – 2nd Edition – Juvenile literature
551.5'55
A full catalogue record for this book is available from the British Library.

Acknowledgements
The Publishers would like to thank the following for permission to reproduce photographs: Alejandro Alvarez/Philadelphia Daily News/ZUMA Press p15, Associated Press pp17, Blickwinkel/Alamy p24, Corbis pp9, 22, Richard Cummins/SuperStock p14, Digital Vision p7, Ecoscene pp19, 28, Damon Higgins/Palm Beach Post/ZUMA Press p18, Oxford Scientific Films pp5, 6, 16, 23, PA Photos pp4, 11, Papilo pp8, 25, Popperfoto p20, Rex Features p26, Robert Harding Picture Library p27, Stone p12, Stock Market pp21, 29, Topham Picturepoint p13.

Cover photograph of snow falling reproduced with permission of Ryan McVay/Getty Images.

The Publishers would like to thank Mark Rogers and the Met Office for their assistance with the preparation of this book.

Every effort has been made to contact copyright holders of any material reproduced in this book. Any omissions will be rectified in subsequent printings if notice is given to the Publisher.

The paper used to print this book comes from sustainable resources.

Any words appearing in the text in bold, **like this**, are explained in the Glossary.

Contents

What is a blizzard?

A blizzard is a very fierce **snowstorm**. It happens mostly in winter. Snow falls from the clouds and strong winds blow the snow around.

■ *Snow on roads and pavements can make it hard to get about.*

■ *This road has been covered by a snowdrift.*

Wind picks up snow from the ground. The snow is tossed into the air. The wind blows it into deep **drifts**. These snowdrifts cover roads and block doorways.

Where do blizzards happen?

Blizzards often happen on high mountains. This is because the air is colder on high ground. Some mountains are always covered in snow.

■ *Some mountains get a lot of snow.*

Blizzards usually happen in winter.

Blizzards happen in warmer parts of the world, too. They happen in North America, northern Europe and China. In these places they happen mostly in the cold winter **season**.

What is snow?

Snow is made of tiny **crystals** of frozen water. The crystals form high up in the sky. They stick together as they fall. This makes many snowflake shapes and patterns.

■ *Every snowflake crystal has a different pattern.*

■ *Skiing is a fun sport to do in the snow.*

Snow falls in layers. Some layers are made
of dry, powdery snow. This is good for skiing.
Other layers are made of wet, heavy snow.
This is better for making snowballs!

Why do blizzards happen?

Blizzards happen when **crystals** of frozen water form in clouds. The crystals get so heavy that they stick together and fall as snow. They whirl down from the clouds, making a **snowstorm**.

Cloud

Snow

■ *Snowflakes fall from a cloud to make a snowstorm.*

■ *A blizzard can make a walk very difficult.*

A cold wave of air rushes in behind the snowstorm. These freezing winds blow the snow all around. When snow is blown by strong winds the storm is called a blizzard.

What are blizzards like?

Blizzard winds make the air icy cold. The thick snow makes it hard to see ahead. Then the snow settles into big **drifts**.

■ *Big piles of snow can take a long time to melt.*

■ *Blizzards can make driving difficult and dangerous.*

It is dangerous to drive through a blizzard. The snowflakes stop the driver from seeing the road. The road gets slippery with the icy snow.

Blizzard in the city

The city of Philadelphia lies in the northeast of the United States. In the winter of 2005 the city was hit by a strong blizzard.

■ *Philadelphia can be warm in the summer.*

■ *It was difficult to travel in the blizzards of 2005.*

The streets were blocked with snow. Aircraft had to stay on the ground. Cars were covered in snow.

Harmful blizzards

Blizzards can stop people from reaching hospitals and schools. Trucks that carry food cannot get to the shops.

■ *This car is completely covered in snow.*

Blizzards make thick layers of snow on the mountains. These layers can slip. Then an **avalanche** of snow tumbles down. This can bury people and animals.

Preparing for blizzards

Weather forecasts can often tell when a blizzard is coming. The weather forecasters give out weather warnings. Then people can prepare for the blizzard.

■ *Computers help us keep track of the weather.*

■ *Snow cannot settle if salt is spread on the road.*

Roads can be prepared for a blizzard. Road workers spread salt on the roads. This melts the snow as it falls on the road.

How do people cope with blizzards?

A **snowplough** is used to clear roads after a blizzard. The snow is pushed to the side of the road. The snow piles up at the edge of the road.

■ *This snowplough is clearing the road so cars can get through.*

■ *It is important to dress very warmly in a blizzard.*

People wear thick coats to protect them from blizzard winds. A hat is very important for keeping the head warm. Boots help people to walk through the snow.

Coping with blizzards – Inuit

This boy is an Inuit. Inuit are people who live in the cold **Arctic region**. This boy wears layers of clothing that trap warm air. He has a fur-lined hood and snow boots to protect him from the cold.

■ *This boy's clothes keep him warm even when it is very cold.*

■ *These men are building an igloo.*

Some Inuit can build houses quickly out
of blocks of snow. This protects them from
blizzards. Inuit can catch fish by making holes
in the thick ice and snow that cover the sea.

How does nature cope?

Lambs are often born under the snow in a blizzard. The mother's body melts the snow around it. This makes a warm space to keep the lamb alive.

■ *Sheep have thick woollen coats to keep them warm in a blizzard.*

■ *This flower is specially designed to grow on cold mountains.*

This mountain flower has hairy leaves. They let in light but protect the plant from blizzard winds. Many plants die in winter. Their roots or seeds lie safe underground.

To the rescue!

In the mountains, trained dogs sniff for people buried in the snow. Rescuers follow the dogs. Then the rescuers push long poles into the snow to find the people.

■ *Rescuers dig for people trapped in the snow.*

■ *This car has skidded off the road in the snow.*

People have to be very careful if they are driving through a blizzard. Sometimes there are accidents and rescue services have to pull cars out of the snow.

Adapting to blizzards

The big roofs of these houses protect people inside from the snow. The snow falls away from doors and walls.

■ *In the winter, these houses may be covered in snow.*

■ *It is important to shelter somewhere warm in a blizzard.*

This is a **snow lodge**. They are built in wild mountain forests. Walkers can shelter inside when there is a blizzard. They can find food and make a warm fire.

Fact file

◆ The northeast coast of the United States gets very bad blizzards. On 12 February 2006, 69 centimetres (27 inches) of snow fell in New York in just a few hours. Thousands of people were stranded at airports.

◆ Strong blizzard winds can blow snow on the ground into snowballs. These are called "snow rollers".

Glossary

Arctic region area around the North Pole. The area around the South Pole is called the Antarctic region.

avalanche when a thick, heavy layer of snow slips down a mountainside

crystals small shapes of frozen water

drift snow that is blown into a thick mound

season months of the year that have the same type of weather

snow lodge hut that shelters walkers in a blizzard

snowplough vehicle that can clear the snow from roads

snowstorm heavy snow and strong winds brought by large dark clouds

weather forecast information about the weather that we will get in the future

More books to read

The Weather: *Snow*, Terry Jennings (Chrysalis Children's Books, 2004).
Weather Around You: *Snow*, Anita Ganeri (Hodder Wayland, 2004)

Index

Titles in the *Wild Weather* series include:

Hardback 978-0-431-15081-9

Hardback 978-0-431-15082-6

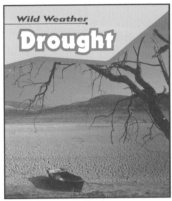

Hardback 978-0-431-15083-3

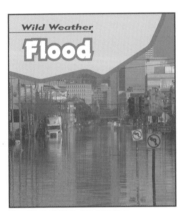

Hardback 978-0-431-15080-2

Hardback 978-0-431-15085-7

Hardback 978-0-431-15086-4

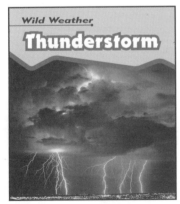

Hardback 978-0-431-15087-1

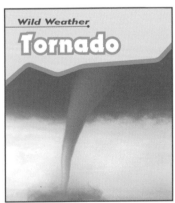

Hardback 978-0-431-15088-8

Find out about other titles Heinemann Library on our website www.heinemann.co.uk/library